ACHIEVING
LIFE & CAREER SUCCESS

"Your Personal Life Success Plan"

Odyssey of Learning

Cloud of Unknowing

Creative Visualization

7 SEVEN STEPS

Attitudes Disciplines

Your Ten Year Goals

Your Path of Life

Define Success

By Dennis J. Sobotka
email: achievingsuccesscenter@gmail.com
Website: www.achievingsuccesscenter.com

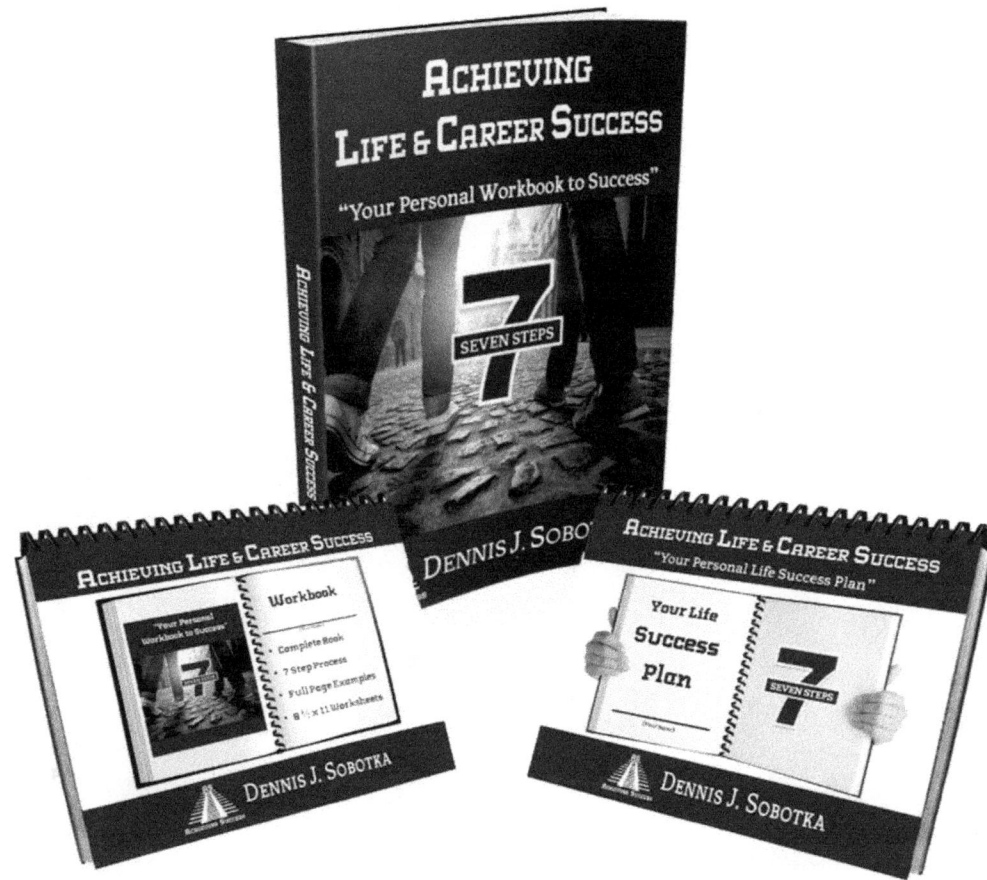

Achieving Life & Career Success Set (Now Available)

The magic of Dennis' book is the 7 step process that provides a specific step-by-step method to create your own customized written life success plan. This personalized success plan is unique and powerful with results that have delivered significant life and career changes.

The Achieving Life & Career Success Set consists of the original book, 8.5x11 workbook and condensed 8.5x11 success plan booklet. These products can be used by individuals or groups interested in using the correct tools to define and achieve their success. Sponsorship of these products by companies or organizations can increase their recognition and involvement in their community.

www.achievingsuccesscenter.com

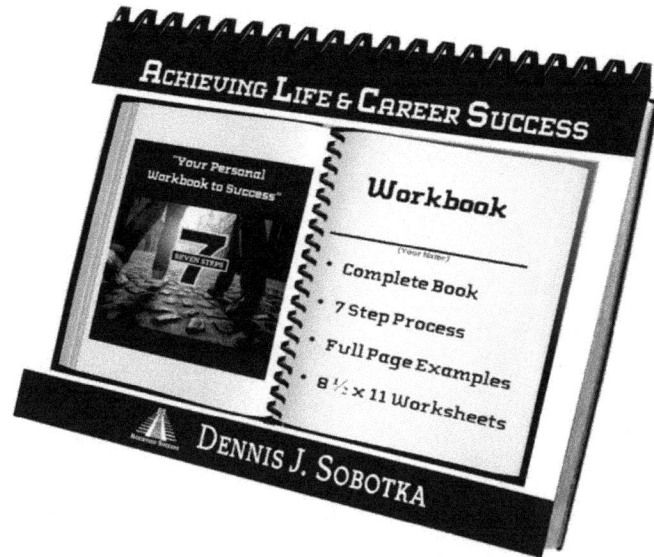

Workbook (Now Available)

The Achieving Life & Career Success Workbook is a combination book and workbook. First it contains the original Achieving Life & Career Success book with the 7 step process for success. Second, the workbook takes you step by step through the text reading followed by the exercise workshops. It provides you with completed 8.5x11 worksheet examples and blank worksheet to assist you in completing the exercises. These worksheets can be used in conjunction with the book, as well as those presented at the Achieving Life & Career Success seminars and classroom instructions. The completed worksheets will reflect each individual's own defined plan for success in their life following the 7 step process. This workbook is effective for both individuals and in a group or classroom setting as it is complete and ready to be used.

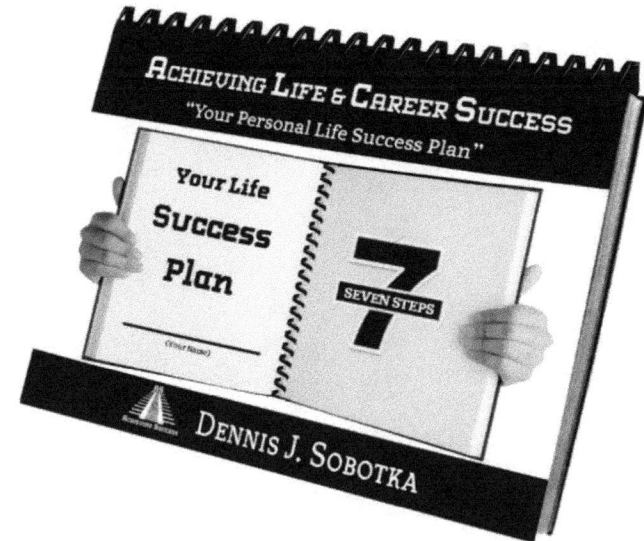

Success Plan Booklet (Now Available)

The Success Plan is a personalized booklet consisting of blank worksheets that correspond to the exercises taught in the Achieving Life & Career Success book, workbook and seminar workshops. When used in conjunction with the book, workbook or seminar, the completed booklet offers you a condensed summary of your own personalized success plan. It can then be easily shared with spouses, family, friends, coaches, teachers, and special people in your life.

TABLE OF CONTENTS

Introduction   **Overview**   6

Step 1   **Define Success**   8
                          What is your Definition of Success?

Step 2   **Your Path of Life,**   10
                          Where Have You Been?

Step 3   **Your Ten Year Goals**   16
                          Where are You Going?

Step 4   **Attitudes/Gratitude/Disciplines**   28
                          Daily Success Tools

Step 5   **Creative Visualization**   35
                          Most Powerful Tool

Step 6   **Cloud of Unknowing**   38
                          Mentors / Role Models

Step 7   **Odyssey of Learning**   41
                          Personal Development

Summary   **Key Action Steps**   44

INTRODUCTION

Our Mission: *It is our commitment and passion to provide individuals with the **spark**, the **vision**, the **path**, and the **tools** needed to achieve their full potential for success.*

You have taken the steps needed for success by investing your time and money into purchasing this success plan booklet, which means you have either read our book, Achieving Life & Career Success, or you have attended our Achieving Life & Career Success Seminar. Both the book and the seminar are designed to share the exercises needed to complete this success plan booklet. Upon completing this plan booklet, you will have documented your own personalized life success plan.

The intent of the book, Achieving Life & Career Success, is to provide direction to all people who are seeking self-improvement and have a desire to achieve life and career success. The magic of the *7 Step Process* is that it delivers a specific step-by-step method to create your own customized life success plan which you write into this success plan booklet. This personalized life success plan is unique and powerful with results that have delivered significant changes in the lives of others.

This 7 Step Process for achieving life and career success can be used effectively with a wide-range of individuals. It is designed to help the non-professional and professional person on their path to success. The emphasis is on individual dreams to success which is why our 7 Step Process is effective with all ages, groups and organizations. Our process has been used by companies with middle and senior management, advanced professionals in their fields of studies, public school and college students, along with community groups and organizations.

The preferred approach in using this booklet is to complete each exercise as you read the book or attend the seminar while learning the 7 Step Process. This will provide you with the greatest benefit.

Let us summarize what will be covered in each of the 7 steps to give clarity of the process.

Step 1 - Defining Success: You will establish your individualized definition of success by reflecting on your personal dreams and desires. This will be facilitated by challenging you to think bigger than your present self-imposed limitations.

Step 2 - Your Path of Life: "Where Have You Been?" This is an analytic review of your past life activities in which you will identify your strengths and weaknesses. These learnings will help to build your future path of life to achieve your dreams of success.

Step 3 - Your Ten Year Goals: "Where Are You Going?" A combination of long term and short term goals are needed to achieve your definition of success. First, you will identify long term goals which will be incorporated into a ten year plan. Then you will establish short term goals directed towards accomplishing your long term goals in your ten year plan. Milestones of accomplishments will be identified along your path towards success.

Step 4 - Attitudes and Disciplines: The theme of this section is to provide you with daily success tools and the required changes needed when using them.

Step 5 - Creative Visualization: This is the most powerful daily success tool that can be used to achieve your short and long term goals which will lead to your dreams of success.

Step 6 - Cloud of Unknowing: "You Don't Know What You Don't Know." This part of the process recognizes voids of knowledge. Mentors and role models will be identified in this step that will assist you in filling these voids of knowledge.

Step 7 - Odyssey of Learning: Personal development is emphasized in this step to encourage your continued improvement in skills that will assist you in completing your short and long term goals. We will introduce the concept called the odyssey of learning in which you will reach out to unique individuals for additional learnings.

The teachings in our book are written in conjunction with our seminar/workshops. Our success seminar called "Achieving Life and Career Success" is a hands-on, personalized approach for individuals to explore their inner dreams and then manifest them into reality. The same 7 Step Process presented provides an individualized written life success plan that is found in all three of our products; the book, a workbook and at the seminars. Individuals from different countries and walks of life have attended our success seminars and completed their written life success plans over the past 20 years.

The teaching approach used consists of three parts both in this book and during our success seminars. These three parts are:

1. Teaching the core learnings.
2. Completing the exercise worksheets based on the core learnings.
3. Summarizing the workshops and engaging in open discussions, affording the opportunity for individual and group participation.

The Achieving Life & Career Success book contains the first two parts, teaching the core learnings and completing the exercises. The third part, open discussions, can be achieved when sharing your learnings from the book with other family members and friends. The benefits of sharing with others is the positive reinforcement that will strengthen your desired success, along with you becoming a catalyst for them to develop their own success path. A word of caution, when sharing your exercises with others, do not allow negative attitude from other individuals to influence your personal dreams and aspirations.

One of the challenges faced as a facilitator is motivating individuals to think "bigger" with their dreams and aspirations. Too many of us have self-imposed limitations that create barriers to achieving our goals and ambitions. You justify in your minds and hearts why you cannot dream for something larger than what is the norm or expected results. This is one of your greatest challenges to success. After reading the book you will be among the believers and achievers.

Congratulations, upon completing this booklet you will have your written, individualized life success plan. This should be considered an event to celebrate and what better way than by sharing your written life success plan with other positive people. By declaring and sharing your goals and plans, you are reinforcing your conscious and subconscious mind towards reaching your dreams of success. If you feel comfortable, please email me your success stories so that we can celebrate your achievements as well.

So let's get started on this journey together.

STEP 1

Define Success

"What is your Definition of Success?"

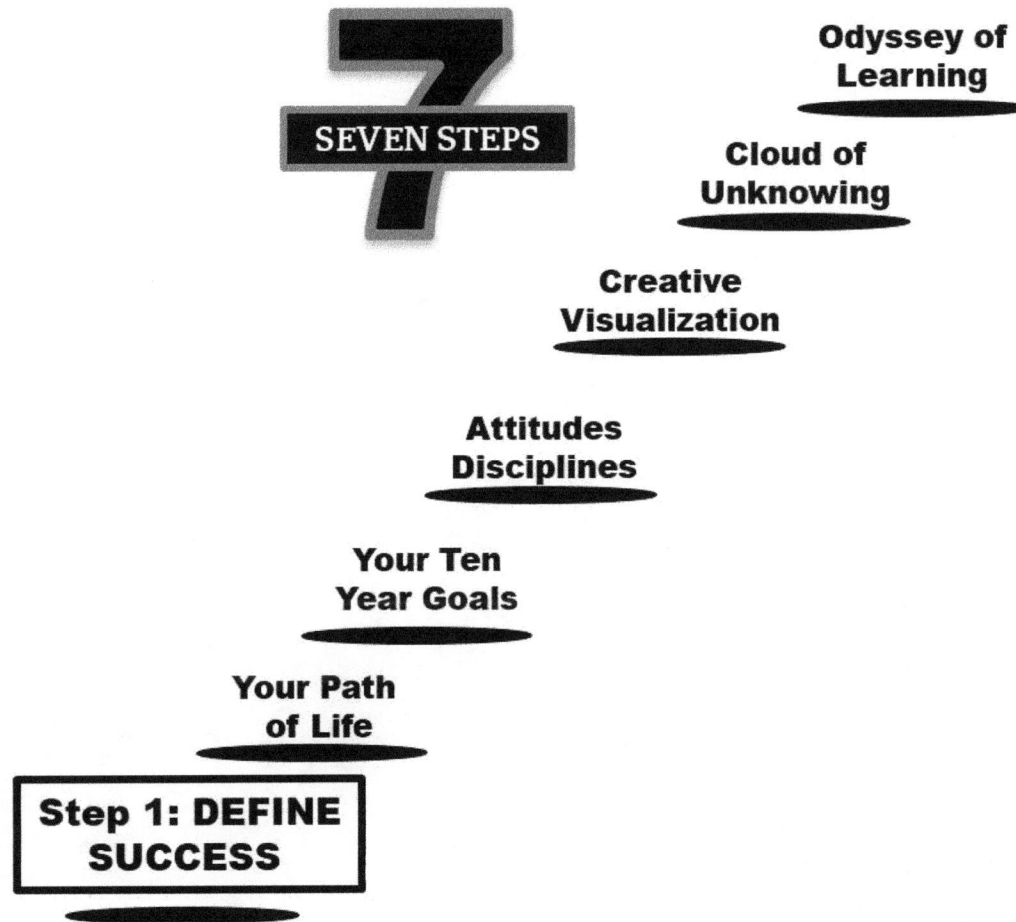

SEVEN STEPS

Odyssey of
Learning

Cloud of
Unknowing

Creative
Visualization

Attitudes
Disciplines

Your Ten
Year Goals

Your Path
of Life

Step 1: DEFINE
SUCCESS

Your Dreams / Your Definition of Success

Your Dreams of Success

Family

Money

Travel

Career

Directions: Record your dreams or aspirations of what you consider to bring success in life. This is very individualized.

_____
_____
_____
_____
_____
_____
_____
_____
_____
_____
_____
_____
_____
_____
_____
_____
_____
_____

STEP 2
Your Path of Life
"Where Have You Been?"

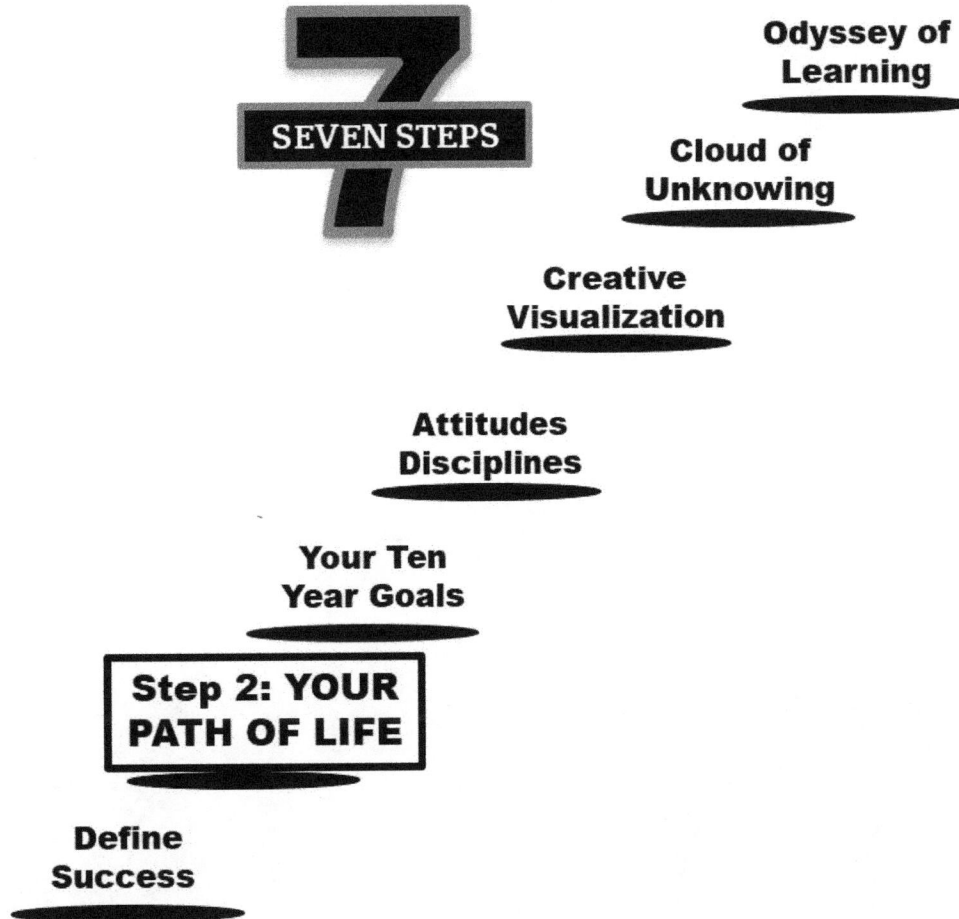

7 SEVEN STEPS

Odyssey of Learning

Cloud of Unknowing

Creative Visualization

Attitudes Disciplines

Your Ten Year Goals

Step 2: YOUR PATH OF LIFE

Define Success

www.achievingsuccesscenter.com

Your Path of Life: Identify your HIGHS and LOWS in Your Life Cycle

Highest

TO

Low

Crash

AGE   AGE   AGE   AGE   AGE   AGE   AGE   AGE   AGE   AGE   AGE

Your Path of Life: Identify your <u>HIGHS</u> and <u>LOWS</u> in Your Life Cycle

Highest

TO

Low

Crash

AGE AGE AGE AGE AGE AGE AGE AGE AGE AGE AGE

Your Path of Life: Identify your HIGHS and LOWS in Your Life Cycle

↑

Highest

TO

Low

Crash

AGE   AGE   AGE   AGE   AGE   AGE   AGE   AGE   AGE   AGE   AGE

Life Observations & Corrective Actions

List OBSERVATIONS (What do you see?)	**List ACTIONS** (What corrective action should you take?)

YOUR Personal <u>SWOT</u>

STRENGTHS: (Internal)	**O**PPORTUNITIES: (External)
1.	1.
2.	2.
3.	3.
4.	4.
5.	5.

WEAKNESSES: (Internal)	**T**HREATS: (External)
6.	6.
7.	7.
8 .	8.
9.	9.
10.	10.

www.achievingsuccesscenter.com

STEP 3

Your Ten Year Goals

"Where are You Going?"

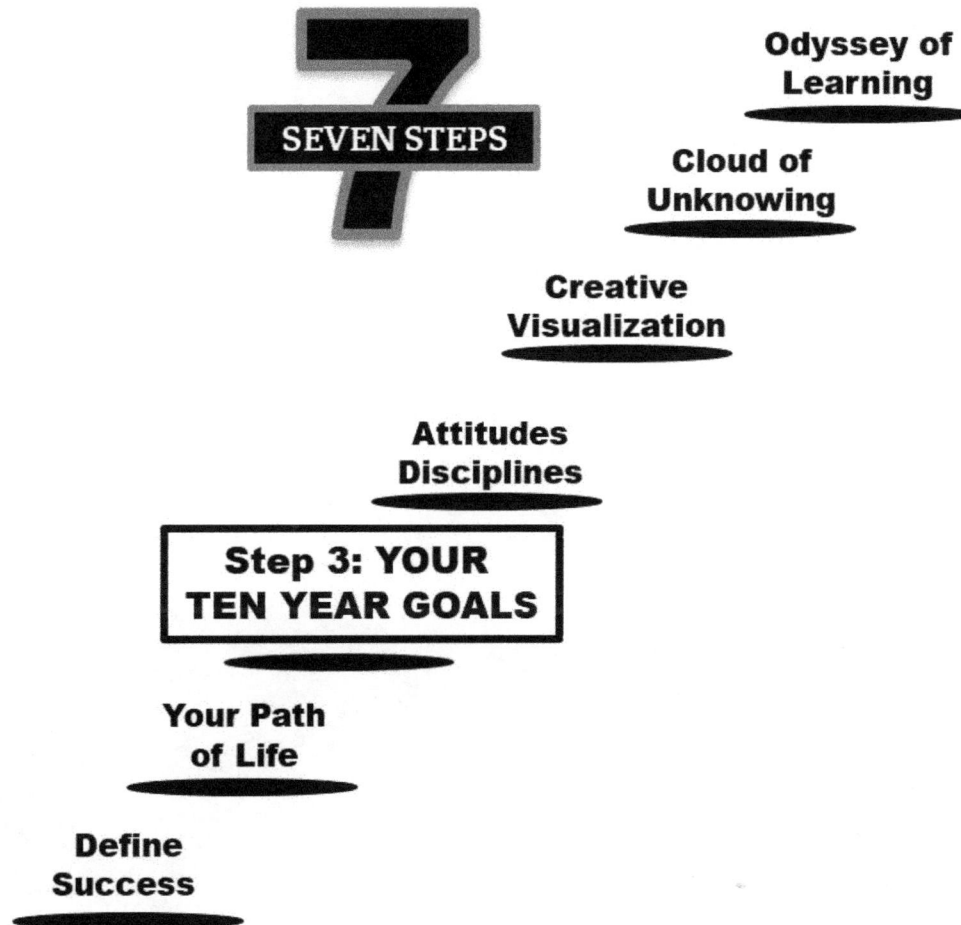

7 SEVEN STEPS

Odyssey of Learning

Cloud of Unknowing

Creative Visualization

Attitudes Disciplines

Step 3: YOUR TEN YEAR GOALS

Your Path of Life

Define Success

CORE Worksheet

YOUR TEN YEAR GOALS

Ages: Years:

SUBJECT	GOALS	WHY	HOW	WHEN (Timeframe)

CORE Worksheet

YOUR TEN YEAR GOALS

Ages: **Years:**

SUBJECT	GOALS	WHY	HOW	WHEN (Timeframe)

www.achievingsuccesscenter.com

EXPANDED Worksheet YOUR TEN YEAR GOALS

SUBJECT	1	2	3	4	5	6	7	8	9	10
Year										
Age										

Copyright© 2015 Dennis J. Sobotka   19   www.achievingsuccesscenter.com

EXPANDED Worksheet   YOUR TEN YEAR GOALS

SUBJECT	1	2	3	4	5	6	7	8	9	10
Year										
Age										

www.achievingsuccesscenter.com

TEN YEAR
Career Ladder

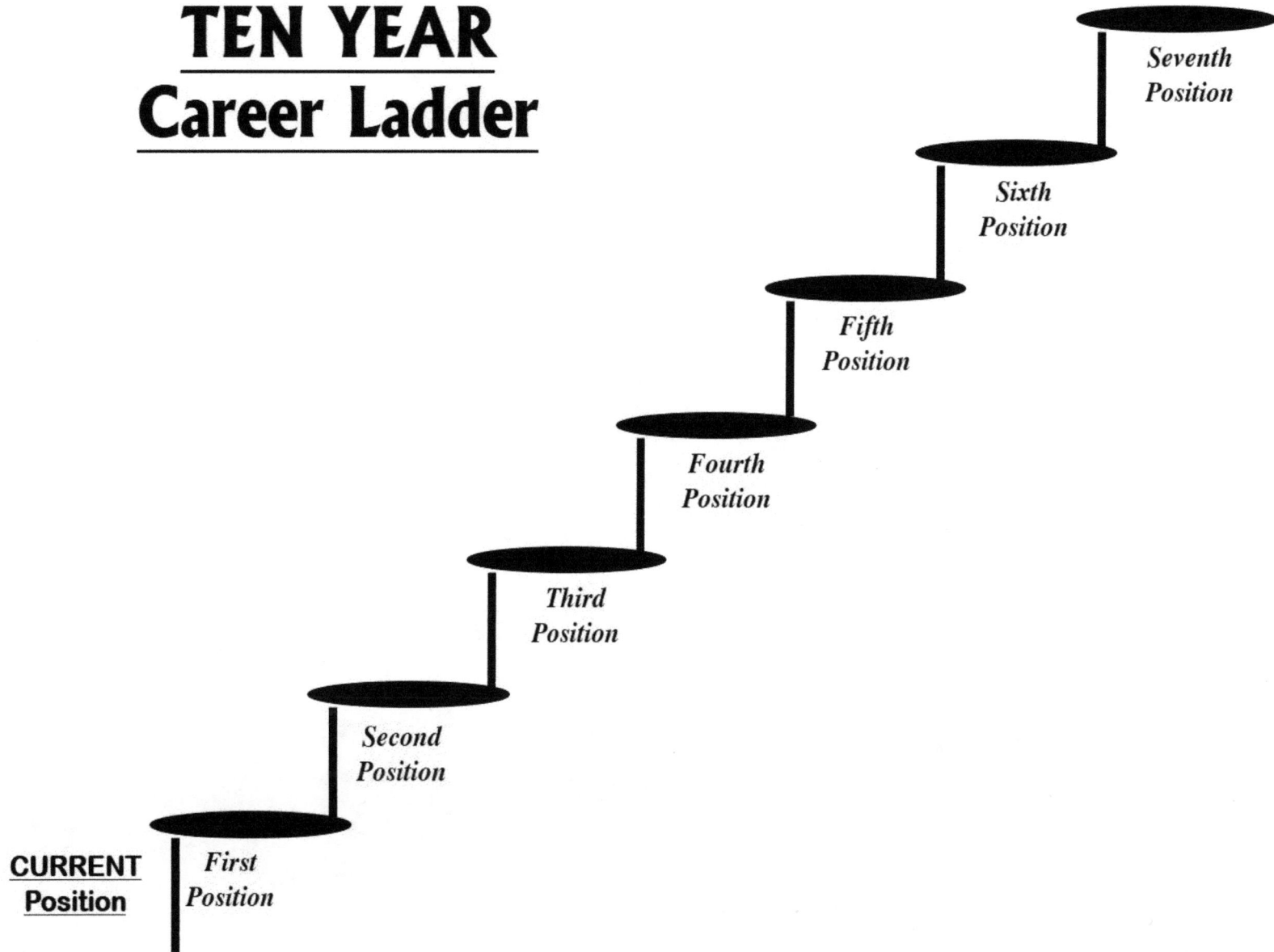

Seventh Position

Sixth Position

Fifth Position

Fourth Position

Third Position

Second Position

CURRENT Position | *First Position*

TEN YEAR
Career Ladder

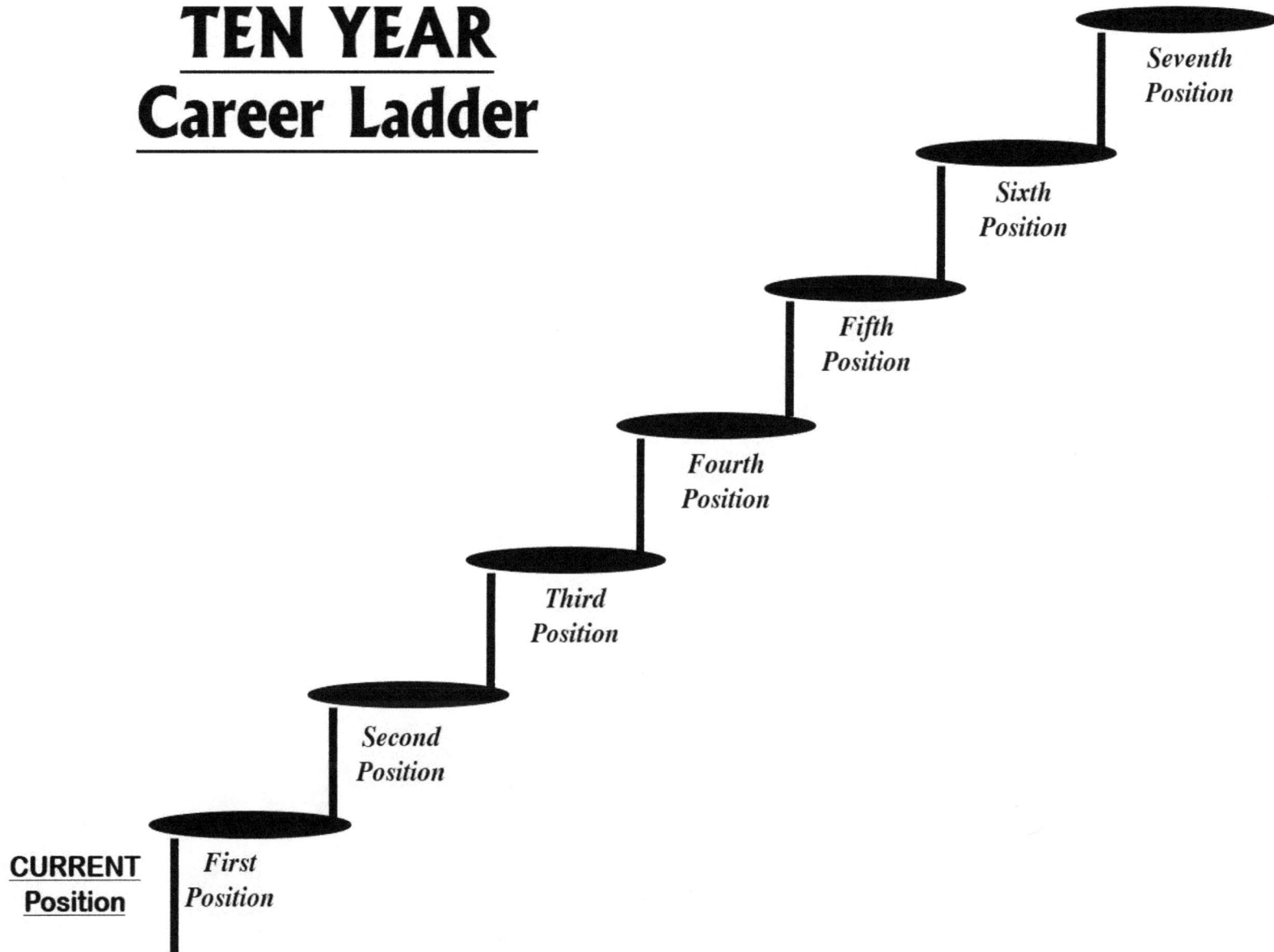

Seventh
Position

Sixth
Position

Fifth
Position

Fourth
Position

Third
Position

Second
Position

**CURRENT
Position**

First
Position

CORE Worksheet

YOUR ONE YEAR GOALS

Ages: **Years:**

SUBJECT	GOALS	WHY	HOW	WHEN (Timeframe)

www.achievingsuccesscenter.com

CORE Worksheet

YOUR ONE YEAR GOALS

Ages: Years:

SUBJECT	GOALS	WHY	HOW	WHEN (Timeframe)

CORE Worksheet

YOUR ONE YEAR GOALS

Ages: **Years:**

SUBJECT	GOALS	WHY	HOW	WHEN (Timeframe)

www.achievingsuccesscenter.com

PRIORITY WORKSHEET / MONTHLY, WEEKLY, DAILY

Priority ABC	Timeframe	Priority by Subject	Activity / How

www.achievingsuccesscenter.com

PRIORITY WORKSHEET / MONTHLY, WEEKLY, DAILY

Priority ABC	Timeframe	Priority by Subject	Activity / How

www.achievingsuccesscenter.com

PERSONAL MISSION STATEMENT

PURPOSE:	
HOW:	
ROLE:	
WHEN:	
MANNER:	
SUMMARY:	

STEP 4

Attitude / Gratitude / Disciplines
"Daily Success Tools"

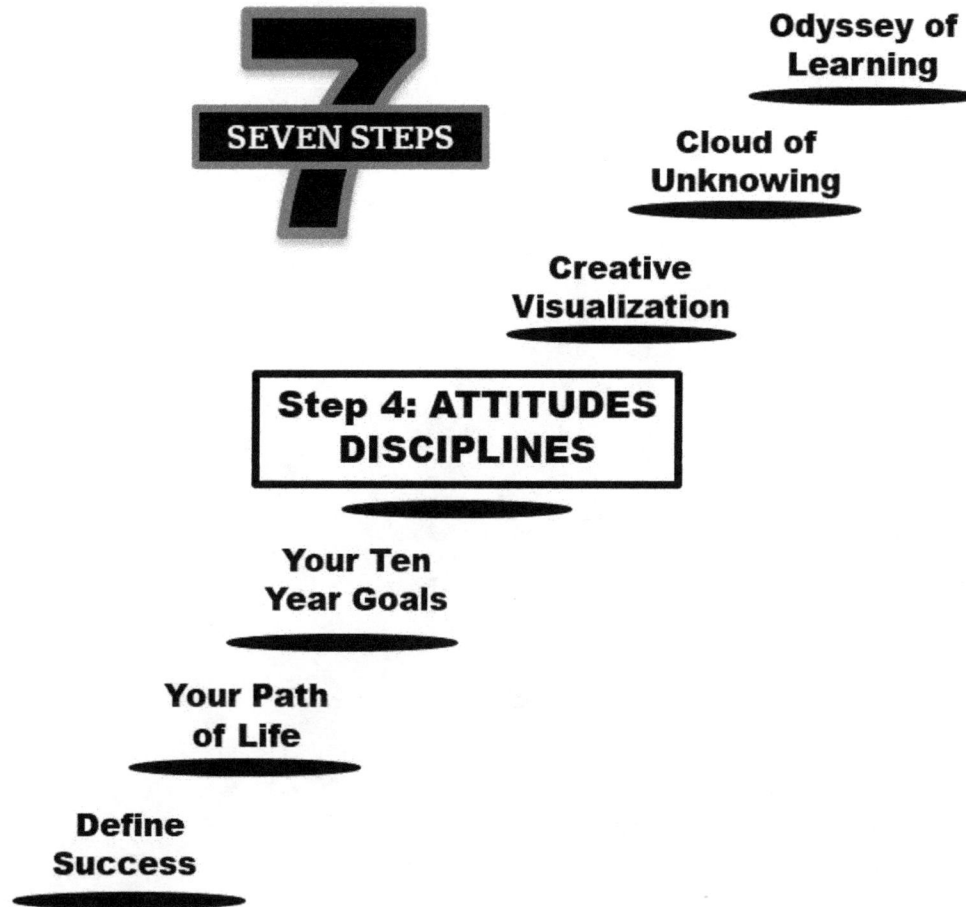

7 SEVEN STEPS

Odyssey of
Learning

Cloud of
Unknowing

Creative
Visualization

Step 4: ATTITUDES
DISCIPLINES

Your Ten
Year Goals

Your Path
of Life

Define
Success

Inconveniences versus Problems

Life's Barriers	Inconvenience or Problem

Attitude and Blame

Negative: PRESENT Attitudes	Positive: NEW Attitudes

Negative: Blaming Others	Positive: Accepting

www.achievingsuccesscenter.com

POSITIVE AFFIRMATIONS

WEEKLY GRATITUDE WORKSHEET

Day/Date _____	I am Very Thankful. Gratitude #1	I am Very Thankful. Gratitude #2	I am Very Thankful. Gratitude #3
Sunday			
Monday			
Tuesday			
Wednesday			
Thursday			
Friday			
Saturday			

www.achievingsuccesscenter.com

Creating Positive Disciplines

OLD BAD HABITS	NEW DISCIPLINES

YOUR DAILY DISCIPLINES

Time	SUBJECT	DISCIPLINE	WHY	HOW

www.achievingsuccesscenter.com

STEP 5

Creative Visualization

"Most Powerful Tool"

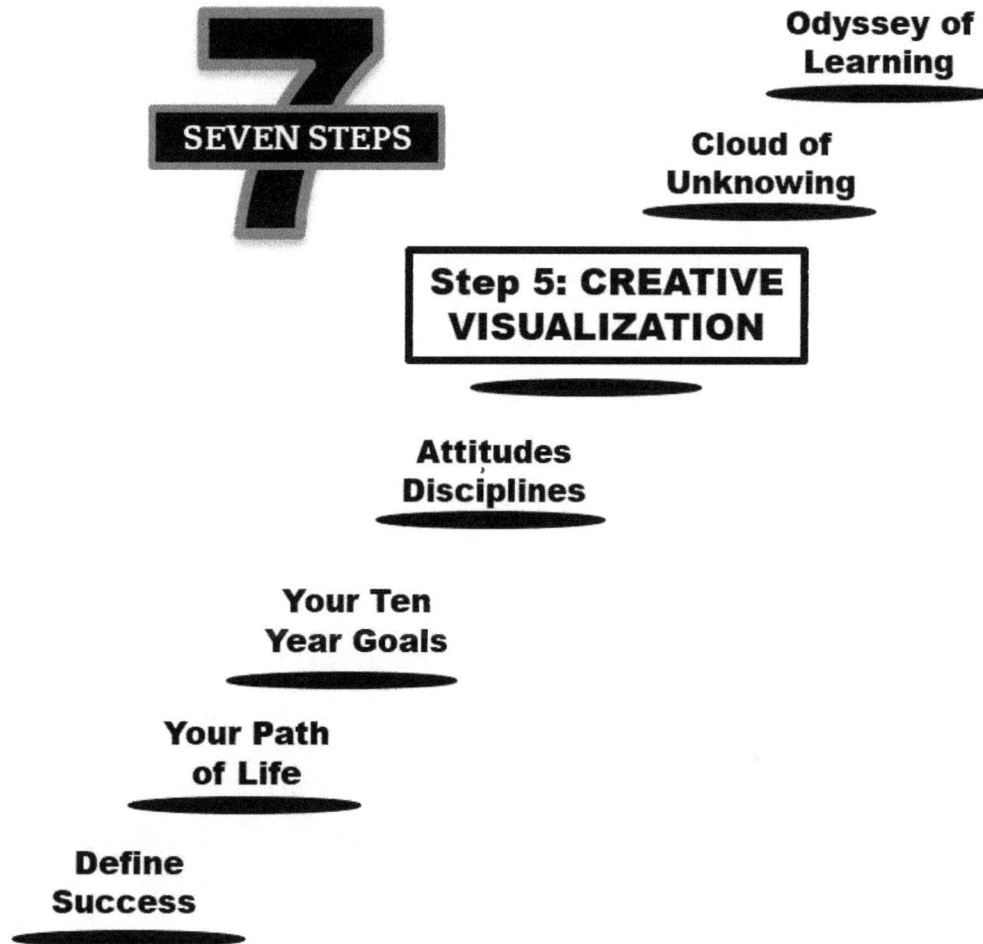

7 SEVEN STEPS

Odyssey of Learning

Cloud of Unknowing

Step 5: CREATIVE VISUALIZATION

Attitudes Disciplines

Your Ten Year Goals

Your Path of Life

Define Success

Creative Visualization

Identify Your Goal:

_____

_____

_____

_____

State what you are feeling and then experience it through all your senses. Your sense of touch, smell, taste, hearing and seeing while visualizing yourself obtaining and achieving your end goal.

_____

_____

_____

_____

_____

_____

_____

_____

_____

_____

_____

_____

_____

_____

_____

Creative Visualization / COMPLEX IMAGE

Identify Your <u>Complex</u> Goal:

_____

_____

_____

_____

State what you are feeling and then experience it through all your senses. Your sense of touch, smell, taste, hearing and seeing while visualizing yourself obtaining and achieving your end goal.

_____

_____

_____

_____

_____

_____

_____

_____

_____

_____

_____

_____

_____

STEP 6

Cloud of Unknowing

"Mentors / Role Models"

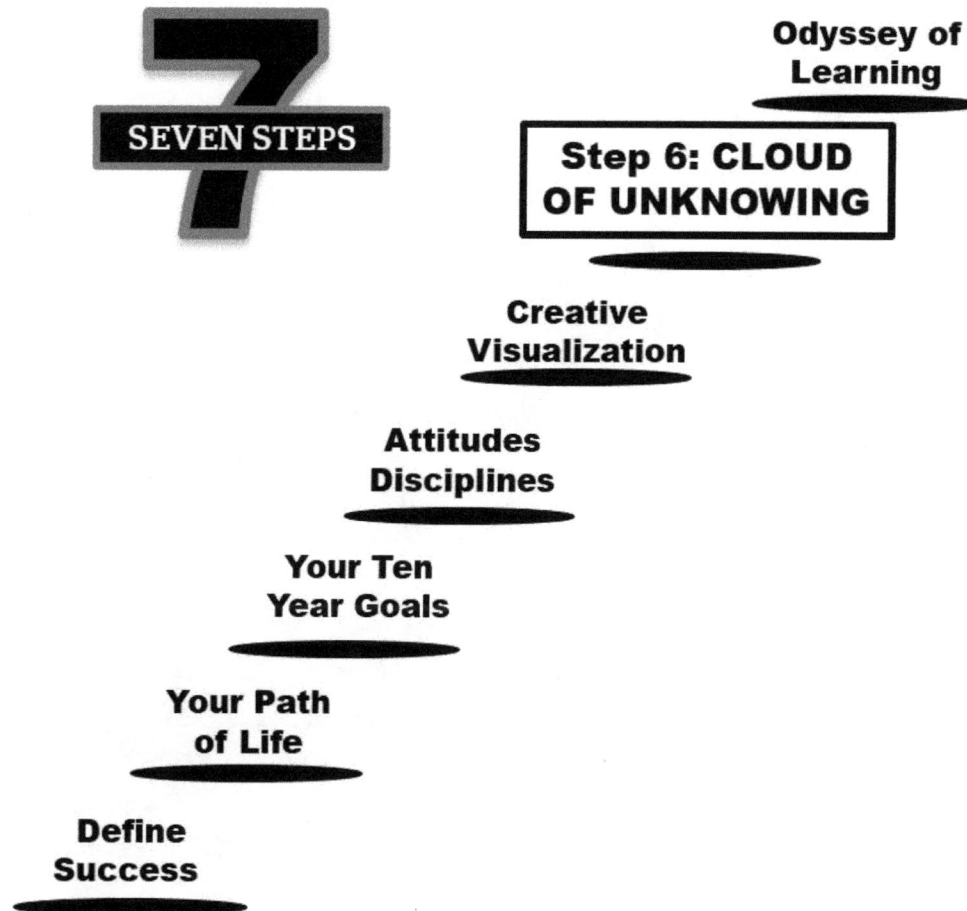

7
SEVEN STEPS

Odyssey of
Learning

Step 6: CLOUD OF UNKNOWING

Creative
Visualization

Attitudes
Disciplines

Your Ten
Year Goals

Your Path
of Life

Define
Success

Past – Current - Future MENTORS

MENTOR	TIME PERIOD	YOUR AGE	POSITION in LIFE	MENTOR'S INVOLVEMENT

www.achievingsuccesscenter.com

Past - Current - Future ROLE MODELS

ROLE MODEL	TIME PERIOD	YOUR AGE	YOUR POSITION IN LIFE	ROLE MODEL'S INVOLVEMENT

www.achievingsuccesscenter.com

STEP 7

Odyssey of Learning

"Personal Development"

7 SEVEN STEPS

Step 7: ODYSSEY OF LEARNING

Cloud of Unknowing

Creative Visualization

Attitudes Disciplines

Your Ten Year Goals

Your Path of Life

Define Success

Personal Development - Timeline

Levels of Development

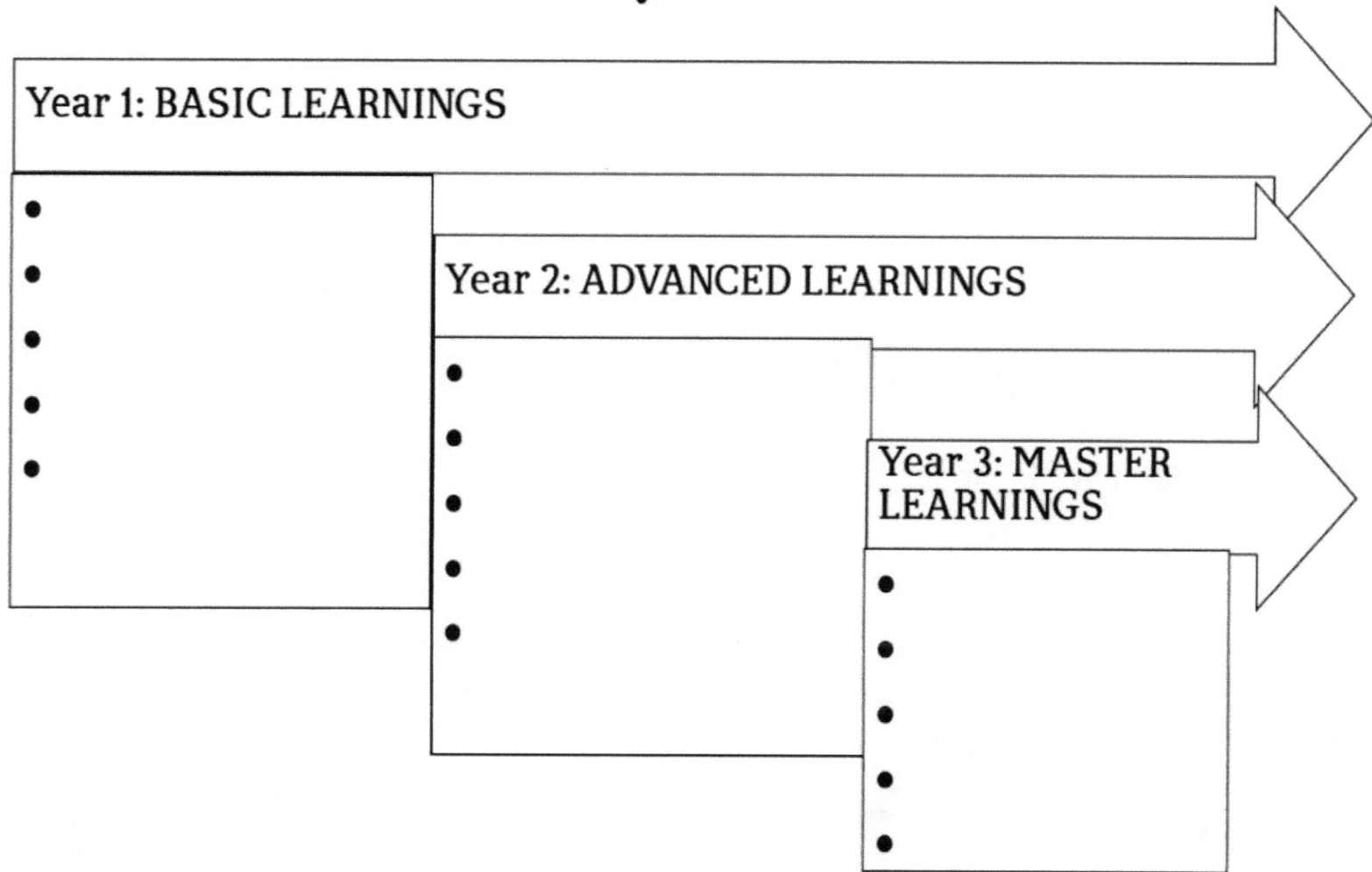

Year 1: BASIC LEARNINGS

-
-
-
-
-

Year 2: ADVANCED LEARNINGS

-
-
-
-
-

Year 3: MASTER LEARNINGS

-
-
-
-
-

Your Personal Development

SUBJECT	RESOURCES	METHOD	TIME	WHY

www.achievingsuccesscenter.com

KEY ACTION STEPS
A CHECKLIST FOR SUCCESS IN YOUR LIFE AND CAREER

If you are not attaining the levels of success that you envision yourself reaching, you may find it useful to review the following list of key actions steps which are discussed at length in this book.

1. Define what success means to you based on your personal dreams.

2. Record your path of life, outlining the highs and lows you have encountered along the way.

3. Document your observations and implications of what you have experienced.

4. Define your strengths, weaknesses, opportunities, and threats (SWOT).

5. Set long-term ten year goals and short-term 1 year goals. Be very specific and detailed.

6. Learn how to manage your time effectively and balance your life by setting monthly, weekly and daily priorities.

7. Write a personal mission statement for yourself.

8. Use positive attitudes and disciplines in your life. Include the positive tool of gratitude.

9. Don't blame others, accept responsibility for your life.

10. Master the art of getting past life's barriers; inconveniences versus problems.

11. Visualize reaching your goals with specific details and including all of your senses.

12. Seek out mentors in your life to become enlightened with the Cloud of Unknowing. Think about who your roles models are in life.

13. Maintain a plan for ongoing personal growth development.

14. Create your own "Odyssey of Learning".

15. Celebrate your achievements.

www.achievingsuccesscenter.com

CONGRATULATIONS

Congratulations, upon completing this booklet you will have your written, individualized life success plan. This should be considered an event to celebrate and what better way than by sharing your written life success plan with other positive people. By declaring and sharing your goals and plans, you are reinforcing your conscious and subconscious mind towards reaching your dreams of success. If you feel comfortable, please email me your success stories so that we can celebrate your achievements as well.

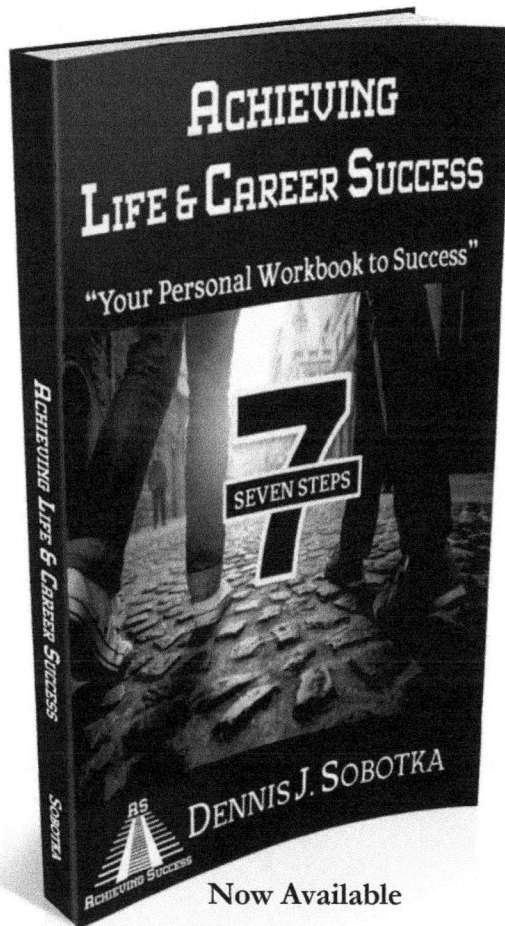

ACHIEVING LIFE & CAREER SUCCESS
"Your Personal Workbook to Success"
7 SEVEN STEPS
DENNIS J. SOBOTKA

Now Available

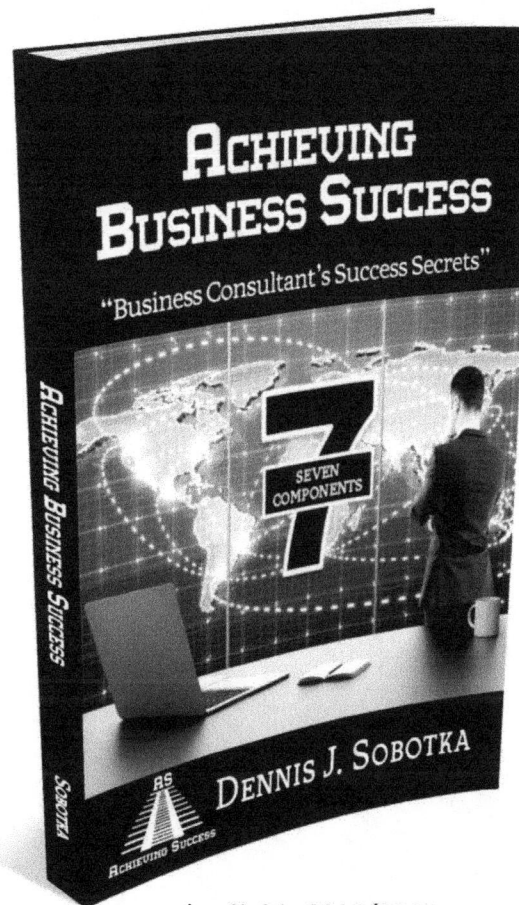

ACHIEVING BUSINESS SUCCESS
"Business Consultant's Success Secrets"
7 SEVEN COMPONENTS
DENNIS J. SOBOTKA

Available 2016/2017

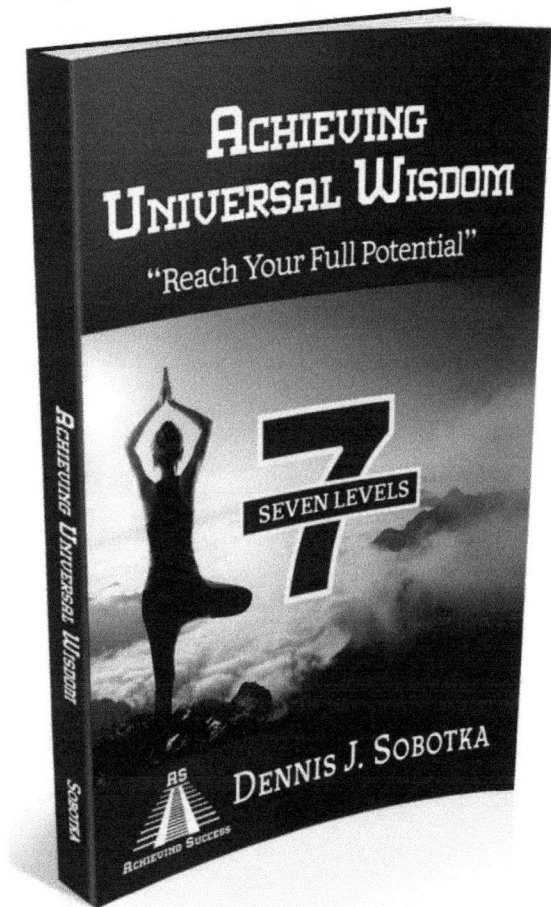

ACHIEVING UNIVERSAL WISDOM
"Reach Your Full Potential"
7 SEVEN LEVELS
DENNIS J. SOBOTKA

Available 2016/2017

DENNIS SOBOTKA

Business Consultant
Author / Speaker
Success Mentor

SUCCESS MENTOR

Achieving Success

Caring Hands

INTERNATIONAL SPEAKER

China; India; Europe; South Africa; Mexico; South America; Japan; United Kingdom; Jamaica; Bermuda; Canada; United States

BUSINESS CONSULTANT

Your Partner In Business

The Partnering Group, Inc.

DIRECTOR of GROCERY

Tops Markets

Email: achievingsuccesscenter@gmail.com Website: www.achievingsuccesscenter.com